THE TELLING OF THE OTHERS

Life with Dissociative Identity Disorder

AVAH RIVERS

Copyright © 2021 by Avah Rivers

All rights reserved.

No part of this book may be reproduced in any form or by any electronic or mechanical means, including information storage and retrieval systems, without written permission from the author, except for the use of brief quotations in a book review.

Disclaimer: All writings in this book are my own and from my own perspective. Names have been changed or left out to protect identity.

Cover by Clover Book Designs

> To all those who suffer, and to those that love them through it.
>
> To the God who holds all we will ever need in His capable hands.

 Created with Vellum

Warning for those with DID!

If **YOU** struggle with Dissociative Identity Disorder, this book may be a **TRIGGER** for you!

Please be sure **you are making safe choices and have support with you if you believe any of this content may trigger any harmful behaviors!**

This book is intended to make others like me believe ***there is hope***! To help you to know **you do not struggle alone**!

And also, this book is for my own journey of personal healing as I continue toward my goal of ONE me.

I firmly believe it is only because of the grace of God I have achieved the incredible amount of healing that I have. Now, I am a very high-functioning individual with DID, and most people would call me quirky and not even realize the truth.

I have learned through hard work, research, perseverance, and self-reflection how to (mostly) maintain a semblance of control over what happens to my mind and body as I live with this disorder. It ***is*** possible to be happy, and I pray that within these pages, you can find some healing of your own.

SP/LIT

THE TRUTH IS, I HAVE NO IDEA *WHAT* THE TRUTH IS.

I fight belief every day. I fight the images, the flashes, the thoughts, and the memories I don't want to think could possibly be memories at all.

They told me it was all in my head, that my imagination was the enemy, that something was wrong with *me*.

My mind tucked all the horrible things away to protect me.

I am Split. I do believe that. I just cannot accept the reasons why.

How could the things I *think* I remember be true?

And my greater fear... if they are not true, then I am crazy after all.

I'M NOT ALLOWED to talk about it.

I write things. Things that don't make sense. They said they would kill me if I told the truth. No matter what. No matter when. They would find me, and they would kill me.

- keep silent.
- don't say a word.
- it's all lies you speak
- nothing happened to you
- you are crazy
- it's all in your head
- only a bad child would make things up like this

You are a stupid, worthless, silly girl who can't do anything right.

The Leap Year

I remembered a rape. The extra night, in the extra day of the leap year. The 29th. The day even the year forgets. The memory hurt. It woke me up, but I was still sleeping.

I was alone. The husband was away. Like it was planned all along.

I remember a man and the pain, but in the dream he never touched me. He was naked and I was young. I'm not sure how young. Not a toddler, but not a teenager either. He was over me, and I knew what was happening. The pain told me, but my mind dissociated the actual touching of our bodies.

I broke. My mind split way back then. And again, in the morning I became one of those splits. I set the memory back, and did everything in my power to keep it back. The emotions hovered. Like the man over my body, the emotions were dissociated just below the surface.

Lurking. Waiting to destroy me again.

I don't want the memory. I keep telling it to stay back, to leave me alone, but it's leaking. Stealing my sanity.

I want to cut. I keep crying. I hate crying. I am barely

hanging on. I want to run. To drive and not stop. To turn into oncoming traffic and end the pain that is eating me from the memory out.

I am afraid they are coming for me.

The Leap Year.

It is bad. Very very very bad.

The Beginning I Forgot

**This poem was written when I was in college, before many memories had come back.

I do not yet see your faces,
    but I know who you are.
    I remember what you did to me.

The memories are still sporadic,
    Hazy and unclear,
    but I am sure of what I see.

The cold air touches my skin,
    and I know you are here,
    violating my body.

My screams go unheard, or denied.
    My terror takes me away.
    The unbearable horror precludes my retreat.

One of you beats me
    One of you rapes me
    The others betray me.

I awake, remembering nothing,
    Until now.
    Until when the story will be revealed for all to see.

Then they will know:
    Why I live in a haze of depression.
    Why I cannot trust.

Why I am afraid to just *be*.

My fault it is not,
    as I was told so many times.
    For it is the fault of those who should have protected me.
    YOURS.
    Not mine.

Born into Broken

Born into broken, the soul must find a way to exist. It finds a story to explain what does not make sense. It latches onto a truth that mends together the fractures of imbalance hovering below the surface to seek glimpses of the world to make its own.

Broken, the soul reaches out and tears memory to pieces. Collides in a defiance of truth that encapsulates trauma into a reel of moving parts clinging to each fracture, attempting to make them a whole.

There is no separation of truth from lie. The lies become the truth. The existence. The memory. The reality of nothing. A lie embedded from the moment of birth that is impossible to heal.

Impossible to explain. Every attempt to sort out the madness inside fails. There is no timeline to place things into context. No order of events that can be examined and analyzed into a past.

A past that never was cannot be truth.

The Whisper of the Others
ON THE OUTSIDE

On the outside, they lived as normal a life as they could manage. They were created, after all, to be an illusion of normalcy. To be a truth the world would expect to see. They were created to live a lie.

A LOT of days I spend analyzing my every thought. All day long I focus on what is going through my head and try to understand why I am thinking about such things at all. It tends to be negative more than positive, and I spend too much time trying to figure out why I can't seem to make my mind lean toward the positive.

It shouldn't be so hard to change the way you think. If you want to think about something, you do. So why then does putting the thoughts you want into your mind not have the desired effect?

If I could only decipher this mystery, then I feel my life would change for the better. Still, the answer seems to elude me. For years. I often wonder if this means my mind is critically flawed. Defective.

IT DOES NOT MATTER how far I am in my healing. I am still fractured. It might be easier if I could hear them speak clearly for me to maintain control, to smile for real, to laugh, to live. But always, always, there is another world playing its scenes in my head. Some of them are so bright they take the smile, steal the laugh, and leave me staring out and wondering why I am where I am at all. Why I left home. Why I did not stay where I am safe.

I try so hard to live. To let things be. To accept that the past is gone and now there is only today. And tomorrow. And the next day.

I am overwhelmed. By the days I have left to portray a self of me I do not even know. The monster inside has never died. I love God, I love my friends, and I love the family I have chosen to call my own, but the monster growls and bares its teeth and I am the one who cannot cross the threshold of the door I need to close.

If I close the door, it is just another secret. Another fragment I have turned my back on so I can believe I am something I am not.

I am not normal.

I am not whole.

I am just not.

Pain

Pain sinks deep into my bones.
    I feel it eating them alive,
    brittle like thin ice… I step carefully;
    afraid to break.
    My muscles knot and hold me in spasms,
    pain sunk in deep; they turn to stone.
    I move like a creature beaten.
    Wary, a long life lived. I haven't aged in years.
    My heart forgets to beat as it should,
    skips of trauma breathed in and held,
    pounding through each exhale; they bring no relief.
    Moisture leaches from my skin,
    drying out like desert sand,
    no oasis to be found.
    My body dies from the inside out.
    I lie down, seeking comfort in softness,
    to ease my bones and relax the tightness that holds me close.
    I breathe, seeking to embrace comfort.
    The door opens and Pain enters.
    It will not leave.

Destroyed
MARRIAGE: ENTRY ONE

THE TRUTH IS THAT THEY (*OTHER PEOPLE*) DESTROY US.

Nothing we do ever puts us back together again so we can live.

I HAVE NOTHING. I take only what I know how to take to survive, and never learn to take the rest.

I hate when you say you understand. You don't. You never will. Your brain cannot even grasp a semblance of the fight that our battlefields, soaked in blood, endure under sword and lance.

Every step forward we take is full of blood and loss. A victory that only leads to battle after battle after endless battle.

I have nothing for you.

I never will.

You cannot look at me and silently resent me for what I am not capable of giving. It was taken from me long before you entered my world.

Left behind to die with my innocence.

What right have you to demand from me what I am not capable of? What right have you, when I fail to meet those demands you place upon me, to hate me for failing?

I don't blame you for it. It angers me, and at times it makes me hate you. Sometimes I feel an overwhelming, deep sorrow for the pain I inflict simply because I allowed you into this littered minefield of faces and feelings and torments.

That sorrow is as deep and horrific as the secrets that hide from me. It has the power to break me. To fracture me into more pieces that I will have to hold together to survive.

I cannot give you more. Nothing more but moments.

You believe I don't feel enough, love enough, or see enough.

The truth is I feel *more* than you, and that is why I protect you by holding back all I can.

I will not see you crushed by an enemy you do not even see or understand is there.

Forgive me.

Over and over and over.

While you place yourself in a position of superiority and you hold onto a belief that you have done more of the forgiving, I am the one who forgives and forgives.

You torment me. You trigger me. You destroy me.

The balance between your hand and theirs is that for them, it was intentional. For you, the dominos fall, every failure I make tumbling another, and then another, until you will forgive no more.

You break me. You cling. You need. Through no fault of your own, you silently beseech me for your needs. They tear me apart. Rip holes of anguish through the already tattered threads held by every breath I take.

I am sorry.

Forgive me, but I will always hate myself for what I do not have, more than you ever will.

DO NOT SPEAK

A HAND OVER MY MOUTH
   Loss of voice
   Secrets
   Stupid
   No one listened when I spoke
   Taught not to speak. No one wanted to hear.

GOD HAS SET ME FREE.
   GOD HAS GIVEN ME A VOICE.
   I CAN speak.
   God has willed it.
   Satan has no authority.
   My voice belongs to GOD.

The Six Demons
MAY 2ND, 2012: THERAPY NOTES

I saw a saucer-type plate with a long, clear tube going straight up.

A woman's hand was sprinkling something into it. Her fingers rubbing together over the substance above the tube.

I asked my alters what it was. Ty said 'look at the woman.'

Child freaked out. Did not want to look.

It was a woman. Old. Long hair. Wearing a robe. Like a witch. We do not know who she is, but she frightens all of us.

Smoke rises up from the tube.

The woman calls forth six demons, three on each side of her; on each side of me. I cannot look at them. They are terrifying. Hideous. Monsters who are too real.

She is across from me.

The smoke was sent to 'enter' me and to steal my voice. *The demons were there to steal my voice.*

I was young. Ty said I needed to renounce them.

I had to struggle to speak.

FOR YEARS, *years*, my secrets stayed hidden. My memories remained locked away. I could not scream. Literally, no sound would come out. *It was not allowed*. Even still, when I am in lost in the throes of a memory, I cannot scream to ask for help. The sound is in my head, but will not pass my lips.

But I *can* speak now. I have. I will. My voice is *mine*.

———

THIS (THE ABOVE accounting) is a memory. A vivid one. I have attempted hundreds of times to convince myself it could not possibly be real. But I see the room. It is dark, and there is stone. It was in a basement. I know the house it was in. I hate this house as much as some of those in my head love it.

I was tormented there. Horribly. I ran away to escape it, but I failed. I was so young.

I could fill pages with things that took place there. All things I have also tried to discount. They cannot be true. I repeat this to myself over and over and over and over.

A truth that is a lie. That's what they said. It is all a lie. One *I* created.

Dear God, if it is all a lie, why will it not leave my head? Why do you allow it to have such a hold?

Because it is not a lie at all.

I shake when I think of this. I fight tears. Rage. Fear. Anger.

Emotions tell you what is *not a lie*.

There was a boy in that basement. He was younger than I was there. I do not know if he was alive, or even if he was real. I only know he cannot escape that horrible basement. If he is dead, his pain is gone. Perhaps in the spiritual world being part of such a ritual pulls you into, he was only there, an unwilling victim just as I was.

There is no explanation. The hardest part of being *this*, of trying to understand your own existence, is that there are no answers at all. I have read the stories of others who suffer with this dissociative disorder. They remember things. They know what happened to them. I don't. I do. I don't want to.

I don't know enough.

I will never know enough.

Or, it is a blessing that I do not, because knowing it all would be too much.

Journal Entry
MAY 2ND, 2008

Today was the first day I have felt halfway decent in a long time.

I kept myself busy. There were a couple of dark moments but I worked through them.

I confronted my parents today about the basement.

My mother said she didn't remember anything bad happening down there but actually suggested that's where the molestation began. My dad said he couldn't think of anything and kept changing the subject.

I don't know what to feel.

If no one knows, how am I supposed to find out? But it was odd to talk to my parents so openly. Even though it gained nothing. So was it open at all? Or just another string of lies?

THE BOX

I am in a box.
    I feel odd.
    A chain is on my wrist.

―――――

I am displaced.
    The air is thick and I can not break through it to the clearing.
    Two alter switches.
    Based on what I see and what I feel, I adapt to the emotion around me. Which one needs to handle the box?
    I find it difficult to move, to stand. My bones hurt.
    My chest hurts.
    Breathing is hard.

Slipping Away

I'm more than half gone.

There are hardly any parts left that want to stay at the surface.

I want to cut. *So* badly. I cannot stop thinking about how it will suck away the pain that is gathering inside of me like a storm about to erupt. I cannot stop thinking about what that will mean for the battle I have been fighting.

Don't do it. I want to. *Just let me*. Some fragment of me says no; you will regret it. The others say they won't, that it will just be one time. I know this is a lie.

It will only take one time. One slice. One rush of numbness to feed the empty blank wall that will fill my eyes and close off my soul with one simple slice of the blade over my skin.

I don't want to hear you. I don't want to see you. I want to be gone.

They scream for it. Behind my eyes they are sobbing and begging me to do it, to please release them from the pain that is hammering against them like shrill whistles in the air that will not quiet.

It has never changed, they are telling me. Nothing has ever changed.

I'm still broken, still lost, still the same fragmented slivers I have always been. We simply found one to push forward that could convince everyone things were different. Deep, deep inside they are not. The roots have never been dug out. The lies are still there. The shadows. The faces. The truth you dare to write vaguely about.

They will hear you. They will see the words in black and white. You cannot take those back. It will be over then. Not their ruin, but your own.

Drown yourself with the slices, silence your soul with your blood.

Do not speak.

You cannot dare. That has never been a lie.

Your secrets are shared with too many because you have not learned the one truth they tried to tell you was of the utmost importance; *you do not speak.*

The silence is your life. The only way to live. Be silent and no one will hurt you. No one will push past the fragility of who you will always be.

You don't have the strength to win. You never did.

You are broken.

Like the title you chose, you tell yourself the truth by admitting it to yourself. You are broken. You are forever broken.

You cannot put yourself back together. Nothing you do will achieve this goal.

The mind cannot split and then meld. It is impossible. You are already gone.

Waiting.

Always waiting.

It will never be over.

Stop waiting for what will never happen.

The one thing you want you will not get.

You will never be alone.

Except you always have been.

One. Lost in a scatter over the ground with a million others. None more whole than the other. Some slivers sparkle brighter but all of them will be swept up and discarded and forgotten.

You too will forget.

Go back behind your walls.

That is where it is safe.

The darkness has always been comforting as long as you don't sink in too deeply.

Find the place where you can close your eyes and exist.

That is what you have always searched for. Not this life you think you need to live. Life will always hurt you. It will never be enough.

The Creator

For me, it is a daily struggle to remember I have a relationship with the Creator of the Universe.

He says I have a purpose.

He says I am worthy.

He says there is always hope and I am never alone.

The greatest truth that has saved my life again and again is that *God loves me*. I can trust Him. Completely. I can tell Him anything.

———

THIS HAS ALWAYS BEEN VITALLY important to me.

There are so many dark, horrible parts of this disorder. Things you would never say to anyone. Never want to feel in front of anyone. I have always known those things don't matter to God.

He allows me to feel whatever emotion I need to and gets me through it.

He still loves me when I am angry, or frustrated, or in a rage. When I am so pessimistic I cannot stand myself. He still loves me.

I am His. No matter what.

Not one single person on earth can do the same thing for you. They will let you down. Unintentionally maybe, but they cannot be everything you need them to be.

If you can believe this, and learn to trust completely in God and let Him walk beside you, hold you when you feel like you are dying, comfort you when you have no hope left, then you will survive.

―――

THE YEAR 2020:

Almost all of the writing in this book is from years long past. I consider myself far along in my healing now, and still as I read and edit this book I am struck by how much further I still have to go.

The year 2020 has been the best I have ever had. I have experienced real happiness, real joy, real love, and so much laughter and peace.

Still, I struggle. I try to be so aware of how far I have come and not allow the leaking of what is in my head to take life from me. For the first time since I can remember, I do not have a death wish. It seems for most of my life I had been waiting and praying for death, and now I am asking God for more time because I understand this earthly life is not all pain and suffering.

There is good. For a little while longer, I pray for the chance to wallow in the good and let the bad stay locked away.

The Spiritual Realm

I believe in Heaven.

I want to walk in it.

I close my eyes and hear the angels singing. To God.

I sing with them.

I feel how the realm we walk in and the spiritual realm are HERE.

I can feel the heaviness as I run my fingers between the two realms.

I lay my burdens down.

The clouds of heaven are the veil.

The power of God is HERE.

I accept. For Your glory God.

I speak for Your glory.

Rend the Realms

I feel HEAT.

Not literal. This world, this air around us is not literal.

It is thick with angels and demons and battle. War.

Close your eyes. You can feel it if you try. They battle for our souls.

Perhaps only I feel it. When the spiritual realm was opened during the rituals I was given a glimpse of the darkness. But the light was there too.

Perhaps some of my selves were created to rend the realms and bring the spiritual world to life for me.

Perhaps it is a gift.

One to remind me all is not as it seems. That behind the surface, there is so much more.

I will not be afraid.

I will walk in the realms.

I will know I am not alone.

God's power is frightening. And *Real.*

I see darkness in other people. I back away from it.

My heart loves until it senses what is not love, what is not pure.

That darkness I step away from. I am free from it.

Am I the only one who sees this battle?

Whisper to me, God. Tell me *Your* truths. I trust you.

Make all of me believe.

I want to cast off doubt so I can trust fully. I want to stand and accept Your promises. I want to know because I know because I know because I know.

The Voice of God.

We are not alone.

doubt

Is dissociative identity disorder even real?

How many could there possibly be of one person?

What really happened to me?

I always feel like something is wrong.

I hate the constant back and forth, the swing between belief and disbelief. The knowing it is true and then immediately doubting it all.

I want to feel something I cannot seem to obtain. Peace.

I want to believe *myself*.

Questions. Always questions. They never end. I ask, you ask, everyone asks.

I don't know the answers.

I stand on one fact: there is *no reason* for me to have created such horrific things in my head. *No reason* for me to lie alone in bed and see the images I see and be destroyed alone.

No person creates trauma so they can suffer.

To Speak
NOV 17, 2011

I want to tell the husband about the DID.

CHEST PAINS.

I knew it was not me. I talked to her (sickness) and told her I was fine and that I was safe.

I told her I do not like to be sick, and that it hurts me now.

I told her about Jesus and freedom and told her she could have it too.

She would not listen.

I commanded her to go. She left.

The chest pains stopped.

Marriage
MARRIAGE: ENTRY TWO

SEP 15, 2013

If I can't embrace me, how can I expect anyone else to?

Do I run away from everything?

I'M BANGING MY HEAD AGAINST THE WALL. UNRESOLVED issues. It is a theory that most long-term marriages end because issues that were there in the beginning of the marriage are still there twenty—thirty years down the road.

Isn't that where we are in our marriage? I am still forced into the head of the household role, still making sure the wheel is turning, still trying to figure out how/why I'm the only one in charge of DOING, of CHANGING.

Grace and mercy only go so far. I've realized that I've continually lowered my expectations of my husband. Lower and lower because I get tired of being disappointed. He only does what he wants to, when he wants to.

If he doesn't want to do anything, he sits on the couch

and zones out and watches people who are acting exactly like he is.

If I choose to do the same, it is with the full understanding that everything I am NOT doing will still be undone and waiting for when I get back to doing.

My children are displaying the same behaviors. The same 'why should I have to' attitude as the male role models in their lives.

I have tried to look inward to see if I exhibit the same behaviors. I don't feel like I do. I run the show. It's really my job. But it is not my job to do it alone.

How can I give when I feel so used up all of the time?

I don't do well with take, take, take, then 'I want' and then the attitude when I say no.

Discouraged.

And then when I am trapped and attacked I say the words 'I feel.' I feel things I am apparently not allowed to feel and then I am told how impossible I am, how difficult I am, how I am wrong and I make him feel worthless and like dirt.

And once again, *I* am the bad guy, the one in the wrong, who requires too much, a monster, a needy, naggy woman who has no right to feel used because he does 'everything for me.'

He shows love all the time, he says. If that was true, wouldn't I feel loved? If he knew me at all, wouldn't it translate?

Then it comes down to 'I just did this for you, and I've been taking care of the outside for you.' Well, when was *that* on my list of needs? Was that above the household that needs to get run? The kids that need to be trained?

He asks me if I hate him? Is this a desperate attempt to make me feel horrible so I'll feel wrong and stupid for feeling anything at all?

Then I'll get the 'you never talk to me,' speech. But

past experience breeds the boundaries. I will react based on how I am taught.

And I *am* taught. Do not say your feelings because the hubby will feel rejected and hurt and like he's lazy and 'a piece of crap.'

So then I *do not speak*.

But I am wrong.

I am cornered and trapped.

When all I have been doing is existing and trying to get back to the place of not caring, because if I don't care, then he can be the same person he has been and not have to change. I know my faults. I own up to them. I know sometimes my feelings are because something has been triggered and I just need to get back to peace.

Forgive me if it takes longer than *you* like.

I am alone. If you can't talk to the person you married, then you are alone.

So yes, he can't talk to me either, so he's alone too. But when does he ever want to talk about anything meaningful anyway?

Why do I even bother?

———

I HATE RED PENS. They look like blood. *(This entry was written in red pen).*

Reflection on Marriage
MARRIAGE: ENTRY THREE

I don't really know what the core issues are. Where all of this rises up from.

Trust? Expectations? Disappointments?

Are those patterns we've created or brought with us?

Just be silent and get through the day. I learned that early in life. I still do that.

My feelings aren't as important as yours. I learned that lesson early too.

The cold, hard truth is, if his needs are met, what I do, and what I feel, don't register.

And that has been reinforced whether he will own up to it or not.

I'm here for the kids, not for him. Because starting over is not an option. Because my daughter is too young, too sweet, too compassionate to break her heart.

The truth is, I *do* love him.

I just can't use that knowledge and pretend it covers everything, because it doesn't. I don't know how to let it.

Love is not a feeling.

It is an action.

It's where you give away, but you have to be full to give

it away, or you're just too busy trying to get filled up from outside sources that you don't need the love from.

You fill the gaps.

You putty them up and hope they hold for awhile. Until, you're empty again.

Marriage and Memory
MARRIAG: ENTRY FOUR

Loss of memory is a gift.

Not for my spouse. The one who remembers everything. And holds it inside and against me. Everything I say is stored. Everything I do is catalogued. My sins documented.

I despise a lot of phrases now.

- "*I get it.*" No, you *don't*, and you never will.

- "*You're difficult.*" This phrase produces a lot of swearing in my head, most of them the F word. You think I'm difficult? How difficult do you think it is *being* me? Being who I am, and married? Having to hold so much back to spare *your* feelings when all I'm trying to do every—single—day, is to not break.

- "*What's wrong?*" More swearing. Are you kidding me? Let me write you a book. The persistence of this question is never for me, only for *you* to feel better so you can stop thinking it's you that has caused the problem. Asking this question causes more problems. Leave me alone. That's what I need. I need to work it out on my own. Not be bothered, and questioned, and resented, and given the status you have decided to place on my current 'mood.' It's not even a mood, it's an actual person living my life for me! But, go ahead, and say you understand again. More empty words to remind me of how trapped I am.

- "*Can't you just get over it?*" Well, I've tried. And tried. And tried. And tried. And tried. Guess it doesn't work that way. Pretty sure it sucks more for me more than it does for you.

- "*Why do you have to remember?*" Believe me, I'd rather not. But common sense, as I have explained multiple times, says that how will I ever figure out what my triggers are if I have no idea *what* they are? How will I ever understand and take control of who pops out to the forefront if I don't even know it's happening? I could go on and on with my explanation for this one, but I'm so sick and tired of having to figure it out for myself, and be your counselor too.

- "*Are you ok?*" Another version of "*what's wrong,*" that I despise. I'm *not*. I no longer ever think I will be. Yet here I am, married and a mother, and the only option I seem to have is to stay in this cycle where I am not allowed to be anyone but the happy, somewhat normal one, because no one can deal when I'm not *that* one. She's not even a forerunner. She didn't even exist until a year ago. She's a background. Without a name. Without an identity. Let me just snap my fingers and call out a fake person just to make you happy. That should work for everyone... but me.

- "*Do you want to do something?*" NO. I want to stay home and be alone. Always. I don't like to do things. I don't like to be around people. I am comfortable alone. Then, I don't have to explain myself, or my body language, or my 'mood,' or pretend to feel or be something or someone I am not.

- "*Why can't you explain it to me?*" I don't often feel homicidal. This one makes me understand how some DID's get this way. I personally do not think 'spouse' and 'counselor' are the same thing at all.

I'm the one that needs a counselor. Stat. Desperately. Alas, no one knows what to do with me. I don't care if *you* get one. Please do.

I've asked, and asked, and asked, but your problems seem to be mine, according to you, and you don't seem to care enough to get one even though I've flat out told you it's what I *need* you to do. That argument always leads to the "*I don't need help; I'm the perfect one,*" comments. Whatever you need to tell yourself.

This is why I lie to you and tell you everything is always fine. You lie to yourself. You just don't admit it like I do. And since you can't handle any morsel of truth I let leak out, what the F do you think I'm going to do? Lying is survival in marriage with a person like me.

I don't blame you, of course. If I was you, I would have left a long time ago. I think you like resenting me. You feed off of it. Off your delusion that my brokenness makes you needed. I don't need you. I don't need anyone. That is the beauty of loss of memory. Of being thousands of different people. I don't remember enough to retain emotion, which makes me dead. I don't even exist. You can only expect so much from someone who doesn't do anything but go through the actions day after day.

There isn't anything else there. I've locked it all away.

To survive.

Sorry this doesn't work for *you*.

Journal Entry
FEB 5TH, 2013

Today I am depressed.

I want to cry.

Last night, I wanted God to take away my boys.

I am tired of their lies, sneakiness, disrespect, filth, stealing, irresponsibility, and laziness.

But what do they see?

They see their father sitting around, thirty-five years old, playing video games in his sweatpants for hours every day. They see his filth, his lack of rules, his disrespect for women and duty and structure. And I let them go there every weekend because I just want some silence.

They see the hubby watching television every day, sitting on the couch while life happens around him and I run the house and do things he doesn't know about, or even care that it needs to be done.

They see him involved when he wants to be, or when they irritate him, or when I am upset, and not before. He's a bare minimum guy.

They see me, a mom who turns away, who is annoyed by them, who barely tolerates their presence. They hear what I want but no one portrays that they should listen. No one shows them what they should be.

They watch the television with the hubby and see men who do nothing but act like moronic idiots, who do not help their wives, who sleep around and talk about women who are nothing but sex objects.

And no one talks but me.

Unless they're pissed off. Unless they feel like getting involved.

I don't have that choice.

I have to be involved, even when I can do nothing but yell or turn away, it's me trying, praying, hoping that I've done one thing right.

That it's not too late.

That they aren't already lost.

Because I see no fruit.

I see no change.

Mom or not, I cannot do it alone because they are what I have always despised... males.

through the window glass
2016

JOURNAL ENTRY:

I have tried to feel sorrow, but the mixture of feelings within me lacks that emotion. It has only been mere days, and the strongest emotion I feel is peace.

He is gone. A good mother should feel sorrow.

A LATER JOURNAL ENTRY:

I've had lots of time to reflect on this. Psychologically, I know I never truly bonded with the child when he was born. I was mentally unstable, lost in my own past of trauma, and having a child was not the best idea. Having a male child made it so much harder.

Emotionally, I have always been withdrawn. Anger is an easy emotion. Anger is an emotion of control. Love has always been an emotion I struggle with. I love fiercely, if one can call it that, but the moment pain enters, it becomes a struggle to maintain. When the pain becomes too great, the person becomes unsafe, and the love ceases to exist.

It is only more pain that the same cycle applies to my own child.

———

2020: A reflection on the above journal entries:

My sons are loved. Their childhoods were difficult. How could they not have been when their mother was a mass of people struggling to survive? I will be the first to admit I did not know what to do with boys. They were a trigger just by being male. And the older they got, the more difficult it became.

I did my best to tell them often I loved them, even when I didn't like them, which I said more than once in reaction to behavior. *"I love you, but I don't have to like you."* No one had ever told me it is the behavior you don't like, not necessarily the person.

Both of my sons now know about my disorder. We've discussed it so they can at least understand. I asked for forgiveness. You cannot change the past. You can only move forward.

I spent most of their growing-up years in therapy of some sort, and as they got older and behavior led to counseling for them too, I was given all kinds of advice.

Every parent has those moments when they make the wrong choice. I yelled mean things at times. Cried and got upset when I should have stayed calm. Reacted rather than processed.

We were advised once to send them to their rooms, tell them to 'reset,' and have them walk back out. It didn't work. Another advised pushups. Lots of them. Hundreds. Goodness, my boys did not seem to learn, and I remember thinking often that perhaps they enjoyed being in trouble. Now, I think they probably knew of the chaos in their mother and didn't know how to handle the constant shifting of my personalities.

My youngest, a daughter, has known of my disorder since she was young. She understood before she realized she understood. She would say things. "*Why do you only like Oreos sometimes?*" Or, literally, "*sometimes you're like a different person.*"

So we told her the truth. I believe, in her case, it has helped tremendously. It has allowed all of us a freedom for me to be who I am at any time, and yes, sometimes she seems to be the mother rather than the child, but she handles it well.

I would not advise this with your own children without very careful thought and consideration. I cannot say if it would have helped my boys settle. I barely understood it myself then.

Today, pretty much everyone I have allowed in my circle knows I have DID. The shifts are subtle and most often apparent in my food choices. I've never been able to get those under control.

My daughter is the only child left at home, and she, and my husband and I, mostly treat the disorder as something funny that we all live with. Not in a mocking way, because we all try to be careful of those who are still broken, but the twenty-five partially eaten bags of chips that get thrown away, or the day when someone puts on a dress (hardly any of them like dresses) are recognizable and funny!

Humor has gone a long way in helping with the healing. If you can be honest and trust those around you, the quirky things aren't so frightening. We think my robot announces "likes," for example. It is very common for someone to say something about something, or I see something in particular, and the words "I like ....." come out of my mouth, almost always in the same tone and modality.

There are still shades to my daily life. Moments when I am with friends and am fine and then I suddenly wish I were alone and home. Moments when I am laughing and joking and then I am abruptly scrambling to maintain the same countenance because the emotions have changed.

I always feel safest at home. I don't care for people popping by and hold a tight control over gatherings in my own home. It is my safe space. I have places that are mine. My chair with my blankets in the living room. My own office that has a couch and a bathroom in case I need to withdraw.

I prefer the blinds to be closed and the doors locked. I don't like lights on once it is dark. I cannot handle more than one droning noise at a time (such as the tv and someone's phone playing a video). My cats are there, always waiting if I need something to hold onto. My snacks are stashed away. My coffee is in the cabinet waiting.

And the outside world, is on the other side of the glass.

TIRED
SEP 7, 2013

I'm weary of being disturbed all of the time.

I am tired of feeling like there's always a pack of monsters following close behind me.

I am exhausted from questioning what is truth.

Forgetting things is draining.

I am always afraid.

I am fed up with always wondering if my parents are good or evil, and if they were the ones who damaged me so badly, or if it was someone else?

Who am I? I'm weary of trying to figure out that question too.

I want peace.

I want to look forward and not back over my shoulder anymore.

I'm grateful I am not alone. God has sent me so many specific people to be there when I am in need. He has truly blessed the journey even if I am exhausted.

What's the verse about being weary?

"Do not...all those who are weary, for I am with you."

I am still tired of it all.

Weary of existence.

Exhausted from this thing we call living.

THE LABEL

WHAT DOES IT MEAN?
Dissociative Identity Disorder.

It's a label. A medical diagnosis. It describes me. It *is* me.

I have lived my life struggling to understand how it defines me and the ways it affects my life. Even if I didn't know what it was then, it certainly explains so much.

To an outsider, it may seem like I am abnormal, or a bit weird, but unless I tell you what you are seeing, you probably wouldn't realize you are watching the way triggers shift the pieces inside of me and become a part of the outer facade.

I don't care what the world calls it. I only care about how to make it stop.

Truthfully, I consider myself high-functioning. I have managed to live a somewhat normal life, despite the suffering I have endured.

My secret weapon is, and has always been, Jesus.

IN CASE you're like me and experienced some SRA (Satanic Ritual Abuse), don't freak out. I love the real Jesus, the one who died on the cross for my sins, rose again, and conquered death. Not the Jesus or God who is spouted by a cult who has told you lies and twisted the message of life and love God holds for all of us.

I believe it is possible for healing to occur without the love of God. You could spend your whole life in therapy fighting and find some happiness.

I believe strongly that if God is in control of your healing, it can become *so much more*. Joy, peace, and true happiness. That your life could be changed, but so will the lives of so many others.

Healing is not easy.

It hurts, and I spend most of my time confused and trying to figure myself out.

This DID business used to run every second of my life. Now, it is like background noise most of the time. It's there, but for the most part, I am always present now, and a lot of the time, I am even content.

If this is what you want, then I must warn you I am speaking only from my own experience. I do not consider myself an expert in any of this. I believe every single individual who struggles with DID is different.

You are unique. No one else is experiencing the same things you are. This is why the journey you are on is so difficult. So lonely. So painful.

Because it is yours, and yours alone. The only One who knows exactly what you need to get through it, is God. That is why He is vital to your healing. Why He has been vital for mine.

I am grateful He has been there for every moment.

He has saved me so many times. Comforted me. Loved me. When no one else could help me get through the next moment, He did.

I prayed for death. Begged for it. Death was my answer for the suffering. Instead, He held me so I didn't end my life, and He has rewarded me for hanging on and allowed me to experience love, joy, peace, and being content.

He reminds me when I forget. The journey isn't over, but He will get me through it. He has proved that truth in my darkest moments, and I have not forgotten.

God is the reason the choices of others that reaped this harvest of trauma in my life have not broken me. He took those bad things and has created good out of them. In me and in my life.

I am better for it. Even grateful because my past has made me who I am now. Strong. Fearless. Determined.

No one will break me now.

If I could withstand all of what was done to me because God was with me, I can withstand whatever comes.

Surrender
SEP 8, 2013

GOD IS WAITING ON US.

If I can break past this lack of discipline for cementing the Word in my heart, then I can break into the truth and the freedom God has always had for me.

What would my journey look like if I allowed myself to fully give my life to God?

I love Him, but surrendering is terrifying. I am afraid of God. His wrath is there amidst the love.

———

BROKEN HAS MANY FORMS. All need to have a place to go.

Pain tells us when something is wrong. Masking the pain only masks what the cause is.

Evil is the cause. People are evil. The world is evil.

Still, redemption is held out for any who will take it.

I accept it.

In the end, I don't want hell. I've been taken there, and I have no desire to ever go back.

I choose eternity in heaven. In peace. Surrounded and surrendered to love and glory.

Amen.

Overcomer

OVERCOMER
 of where I was.
 I bear scars that forever remind me of Who I was,
 A constant reminder that I have been delivered, that I was held in love, and that I was Chosen to:
 OVERCOME.

NAMELESS SYSTEM

A DISTINCT LACK OF EMOTION. A DIRECTOR THAT TELLS you what to do and when to disappear. How to avoid. Avoidance is key here. Don't interact, don't talk to anyone. Just start the to-do list. Clean something, feed people, run errands.

Interaction triggers bad emotions. Which is why we are trying not to feel any. Anger. Hatred. Irritation. Rage. None of which should be brought forth. Those around us will regret it, but we will forget. When this system fades back, so also will most of the time.

Arguments will ensue about what is 'expected.' We are supposed to do this today, but we should not. Anxiety will ebb and flow. Low grade nausea will result during the time this system spends in the outside.

Do not speak. Filters are not engaged well with this system. You must be mindful of other's feelings, even though we really do not care. We want nothing more than for everyone to go away so we can shut down.

Ultimately, that is the goal:

- Rest.
- Quiet.
- Darkness.
- Peace.

The One Born

She died quite young. Not her body, but her mind. She was simply too innocent to handle the horrific evil of the world that is lived under cover of darkness, secrets that easily destroy minds not created to contain such wickedness.

To live, she became two, and then another, and another, and another, until her mind became a hall of doors that would open with only certain keys. Keys held on a ring of triggers.

A scent. A word. A voice. A face. A touch.

So broken, the one born died to live. Others took her place, responded to her name, but gave themselves their own identity. Their own purpose, even if it was only a simple base.

A complex system that began out of mercy, but in the end bled and melded together, became broken themselves, and ceased to know how to exist as the world expected.

They began to hide behind their doors, and another was created to lock them in as they became too broken to lead.

Another floor was built. Another caretaker created.

Layer upon layer, mashed together with whatever was available to hold it all together.

She's buried in there somewhere. Don't look for her. No one ever goes down that deep. It isn't allowed.

The Story of Them
2019

I FORGOT MY LIFE.

During the trauma, I very effectively created alter after alter to handle everything. Every emotion. They endured the pain. They looked into the eyes of our abusers. They took it all.

I forgot.

It enabled me to survive.

I am grateful. And other days I am annoyed. It is difficult to not remember. It makes you feel crazy. Like you're making things up that can't possibly have happened.

Worse, because I created alters to handle the emotions, even if I do remember, it's like a blip. An "okay, whatever" moment that doesn't even seem real because I don't feel anything when I think about it. That makes me feel crazy. Like there is something wrong with me.

The truth is, I am normal. It's just my own version.

I have learned the greatest moments of pain have brought great healing. Each one of my pieces must heal from their pain. Our pain.

The problem with that scenario is that in order for it to

happen, they must be allowed out, and to feel the pain again. You must be present enough to feel it as well, and to speak to that part of you, pray for both of you, and allow God to hold your hand as you process the trauma that occurred so it will stop controlling you.

That is what trauma does. It controls you, until *you* learn to control *it*.

Hiding it in the secret parts of your brain does not help you. Life is a ticking clock of triggers, and eventually, a trigger is going to unbolt the lock you have around a memory and force it to the surface, and you will react.

The sections of the story you remember may be incomplete. It might seem like it was nothing and you might not understand why it has affected you for so long. Or, it might be horrific and make you want to crawl into a hole and die.

For me, a part of my story was some form of a cult. They tortured women. Cut them up into pieces. Buried them. Cut the eyes out of babies and ate them. Buried children whole and alive.

They made human sacrifices. Burned incense. There were drugs. Sexual abuse was rampant.

Death. So. Much. Death.

Lies.

The foundation of all abuse is built on lies.

- "This isn't happening to you."
- "You're making this up."
- "This is all in your head."
- "You deserve this."

The cult spoke its own lies. Rooted in their version of God. A twisted evil that took what was good and did everything possible to destroy any chance I would ever find the power of the true God.

The Bible says: "God loves you."
A cult says: "If God loved you, this would not happen."
The Bible says: "You are worthy."
A cult says: "Suffering is required to be worthy."
You have to identify the lies to heal from them.

———

EVEN NOW, I see sharp blades running over skin. On good days and bad. Not as strong as the images used to be, but they linger, taunting me, reminding me of the past.

I cry for them. The ones still lost in pain and suffering. Who took the trauma for me so I could live. I hope the diminishing of what used to be the constant witnessing of blood spilling from cuts means they are finding peace.

It is easier now to close a door and not automatically turn the lock. To strip off my clothes and get into the shower and know I will see no blood going down the drain. I still don't know if the blood was mine or if it belonged to someone else.

I can go outside now and I don't worry someone is waiting to take me back. Or waiting to ateal my children for sacrifice.

I am hardly ever afraid to look in the mirror anymore. I know when I am me and when I am not.

The little ones love certain things. Specific foods mostly. Cuddly stuffed animals. Soft pillows. They all seem to love blankets. Cats. I try not to deny them, even when holding a stuffed animal at my age is silly. It isn't to them. The soft texture and body makes them feel safe.

I let them write. They live in these books. Their stories are in the words. Partial realities I don't really understand.

Sometimes as my fingers fly over the keyboard, I cry. I feel their pain. I do my best to give hope back to them. To show them we are safe now.

Free.

TRIGGERS

1

A SYSTEM

My alters had one purpose. To help me survive.

I gave them no names for the most part. It was easier that way. Easier to keep the secret. Even from myself. They did their jobs, I grew up, became a grown up, and did all the things you're supposed to do as an adult.

Get a job. Get married. Have children. And all of that means: triggers. *Hundreds* of triggers.

Abused by a man? Your husband will trigger things. Your sons will trigger things. A random man on the corner will trigger things.

Abused by a woman? Your mom will trigger things. Your mother-in-law will trigger things. Your daughter will trigger things. Your sister. Your Pastor's wife. Your female co-worker.

Did a ritual you were involved in happen in the woods? Going camping will trigger things. Taking a hike will trigger things. The tree outside your window will become your enemy.

Did the cult use words from the Bible to achieve their evil deeds? Church will trigger you. Scripture will trigger you.

Talking to others who were abused will trigger you. Watching TV will trigger you. Songs will trigger you.

Are you understanding? Triggers will be everywhere. You must learn to identify them to heal! It is a difficult task. But necessary.

It will seem impossible. It is not.

Ask God to show you what they are. He loves you and He wants you to be healed and happy.

Satan wants you to be miserable and broken. Satan will try to make you feel hopeless. Satan will want you to get frustrated and give up. Satan will do everything in his power to make you feel afraid and retreat back into your safe, comfortable alter-rotation.

Process that.

If you're where I used to be in my journey, rotating through alters means you forget a lot, you miss appointments, you don't want to be with anyone, you upset a lot of people, you have very few friends, and you spend most of your time depressed and wishing you would die.

That is exactly what Satan wants! If you aren't living, you can't fulfill your purpose. And yes you have one!

God created YOU for great things. If you will choose Him, He will lead you into life and hold your hand while you heal.

There are so many others like us. Who need to hear the truth. The world is creating more broken people.

When I began my healing journey, I didn't believe living any semblance of a content life was possible. It is.

I am living it now.

2

TRIGGER: Going Outside
SEP 12, 2013

Having a lot of irrational fears.

I am afraid of getting shot by people walking by me, or even when stopped at lights. I'm afraid if I am window-to-window with another driver they are going to shoot me. I know in my head this is odd, but I still keep thinking it.

Dreams are still happening. I'm so used to nightmares now they don't even seem like nightmares. I'm aware that they are and they are NOT pleasant, but they've become so commonplace I barely blink an eye.

——- keeps telling me to write them down but I'm not sure if I'm not because I don't want to examine them too closely, or if it's because they're just normal for me now.

3

TRIGGER: The Shower
FEB 12TH, 2013

Considering I don't even like to shower, it always disturbs me when I feel the overwhelming *need* to shower.

Yesterday and the day before I felt I had to take one in the afternoon... also not normal. We shower in the morning.

Apparently, February is a difficult time for DID's, starting on the second day of the month.

I would say I've definitely been having issues since about then.

———

SO I'M STANDING in the shower yesterday and I'm going through the rooms in all of the houses we lived in when I was growing up, looking for where every room was located. Typically, I just focus on basements, so this was new.

I had an extremely difficult time remembering the order of moves, which house was when, or even if I'd remembered all of them. Then, I got to the town of B———? No, the town of M———. I can't find the bathrooms in them at all.

And I dissociate... I'm gone. Hands down at my sides, feet turned in, the colors gray and wavy, and I cannot come back.

I panic.

I can't find the bathrooms!

Still today, I can't find them.

I realize I also have complete blanks on other rooms. The Aunt's room in ———. My parents room in M———. The younger brothers room in M———-.

I felt physically ill and honestly thought I was going to vomit. I just kept thinking the kids were in the other room and I couldn't start screaming in the shower.

I texted S———. I'm sure she prayed. R——— was coming over so I cleaned, got dressed, did all that.

I was cutting veggies for dinner and having a hard time staying present. I felt dizzy, like someone was trying to force themselves out, to take over. Nausea came and went and I was on edge and struggling to act normal. No need to freak R———- out.

The room thing... is it dangerous to try and figure it out?

'We are doing it anyway.'

———

FOLLOWING this journal entry are maps of every house we lived in while growing up. First and second floors, some rooms labeled, with the age I was at each location listed at the bottom.

4

TRIGGER: Family Contact

THE BROTHER

THE LITTLE BROTHER TEXTED ME.

Said he was attacked by an entity.

He said there have been other strange things he tried to write off because they don't really exist. Like ghosts.

He does not remember any specific abuse as a child.

But he said "...discarding too many things that I refused to accept because they didn't make logical sense."

5

TRIGGER: Sound

I HATE THE NOISE.

The television, the kids, the dishwasher, the screaming, the fighting. It makes me want to cover my ears and scream.

I hate it at work too. That stupid ——— speaker above my head. It took me months to get them to turn it off. I hate the noise of the bathroom, the phones ringing, people talking and laughing, ———'s voice. I hate it.

I like the fan and the sound of my own music because I know I like what I play. That I have *chosen* it because it will not make me crazy and want to scream.

———

THEY WON'T SHUT up tonight.

The daughter crying, the boys stomping down the hall, fighting, scraping pans in the kitchen, talking, a whine in their voices.

The noise never STOPS. None of it stops.

The television is always on. The dishwasher and the

dryer. The guitar. The kids talking. Traffic. The ringing in my ears. The hum in the background.
　I JUST WANT IT TO STOP.

6

TRIGGER: Reality
JAN 2ND, 2013

Television show: '*Law and Order: SVU*'

I've been watching every episode to understand, or trying to trigger something, I don't know.

Last night I watched one where the mother abused a girl. This is the first out of the hundreds I have watched that disturbed me. I was anxious. I had some tea. I tried to determine what specifically bothered me.

The mother. It was sexual abuse that led to severe emotional trauma (in the show).

Really, the only explanation that fits, after watching show after show after show about rape, father abuse, neighbor abuse, etc, is that it is highly possible it happened to me.

Which I already thought was possible. I just have no memory proof.

Since I cannot remember, it cannot be true.

It is easier that way.

7

TRIGGER: Physical Intimacy

They came upon me before I even understood,
    Taking what was not theirs to take,
    Leaving behind an empty, lost shell.
    The air is cold upon my bared skin,
    My eyes are trained on some focused oasis,
    seeking to escape from this forced hell.
    The memory is left behind when it is over.
    Commanded to retreat down an unknown path in my mind.
    Always, they rise to haunt me again,
    with questions whose answers no one will tell.
    One by one, some trigger sets them free.
    I am screaming at the ghosts who escape,
    urging them to stay repelled.

And, I hate you,
    all of you,
    you who abused me,
    who betrayed me.

8

TRIGGER: A Song
NOV 16TH, 2011

I HAD THERAPY TODAY.

I do not know which alters were there.

I do know the others were determined to do nothing more than allow a scraping of the surface.

We talked about a song that had triggered me: Never Alone.

While driving home one night, this song had come on and an alter had come out and taken over. The song was played on repeat for the entire ride home. It was dark. I drove, almost in a trance, with my eyes straight ahead, feeling as though I was nothing more than a shell.

―――

JOURNAL ENTRY:

Driving home from a movie.

Never Alone began to play.

Switch.

Hunched over, both hands on the wheel, we play the song over and over and over, all the way home.

Hyperfocused on car lights in front of me. Glaring

almost. I talked to her in my head. She would not speak out loud. I asked her name and what the trigger was?

I wanted to know what she wanted.

I wanted to know *why*.

The trigger: Never Alone. Something in the music? The words of the song?

Because I am never alone. I am not one.

WE TALKED about this entry in therapy. We prayed about it. Asked God if there was more I needed to know or to see.

I saw a cult symbol in fire. An odd triangle shape that did not close, the line along the bottom extending past where the triangle should have met to continue.

There were blood red candles. Red wax dripping that looked like blood.

I wanted to cry. I was overwhelmed and wanted to leave the room to scream.

We read a prayer meant to address the cult aspect. It was very difficult to read. There was definitive switching as I read. They (at least four or five of them) did NOT want me to say the prayer.

One was a Watcher.

I think she might have been the one who drove us home the other night while the song played. She watches for evil and those that are trying to control me. Others were children. They wrote stuff on the prayer paper.

None of this makes sense.

9

TRIGGER: The Dark
THE DAY THEY LIVE

Cammie 11:53 pm

Trigger: The Dark

I don't understand why she won't just let me out. She fights me, like I'm going to hurt her, but she should know I won't. I'm her creation, after all. Maybe it's because she doesn't know me, and doesn't remember what I know. I guess it all leaks out somehow, tiny little trickles that invade the spaces of the others. I try really hard not to let anything free, but my pain is so much greater than hers is.

She doesn't like the dark. It's my job to handle it. There are others with the same purpose, but I'm stronger than they are. It's better for me to push forward and let her close her eyes and sleep. I won't let anyone do anything bad. I'm stronger. If she could just see that…

The night is like prickles poking along your skin. A prickle, and you brush it away. Over and over and over until light finally starts to seep back into day. I don't like the prickles either, but I'm consistent at brushing them off.

I'm always so tired by the time morning comes that I can't stay forward any longer.

There's so many of them. Triggers are rampant at night. There's so much darkness, and that alone is one of the biggest triggers we all fight. I've learned not to close my eyes. It's easier not to remember if your eyes are open and you can see through the haze of darkness once your eyes adjust.

I don't see the shadows the others do. Just the color of night. She hates the light when she sleeps, so I find those places where it leaks in. The sliver of curtain that is parted at the bottom of the door. The dim light from the wall socket in the bathroom. The glare from the alarm clock that the husband only partially covered up.

I focus on those when I feel them really start scrambling around inside. A lot of them hate the light when it's supposed to be dark. That doesn't make any sense to me. If they are so afraid of the dark, why don't they want the light? I can't figure it out. My only thought is that they are afraid if there is any light they will see what they fear.

I'm strong. I can handle it. I'm the strong one. I'm the strong one. I'm the strong one.

―――

ALISA 3:43 am

"Hush little baby don't you cry. If you cry then you will die."

I'm so afraid. I can't stop shivering. I thought I heard a noise, and I don't think I am alone anymore.

I want to close my eyes but I can't... I need to see, I have to know for sure if he's coming...

―――

CASSANDRA 3:49 am

If I think about everything I didn't do during the day, then I won't remember it's dark. I didn't do anything. Didn't clean, or tidy up the living room. I was going to read, but I didn't. I didn't even get dressed. I was going to do all these things, have a good day, accomplish something. Instead, I did nothing. I'm such a failure.

Why can't I ever do what I really want to do? If I could just organize my life, it would be so much better.

I should be productive now and figure out what we are going to wear tomorrow. It's so irritating to pick out clothes. I should have looked to see what the weather is going to be. Why didn't I do that? How many times do I go to bed and have this same thought process? I can't even check the weather and get that right!

Maybe jeans. We all love jeans. Except it's supposed to be hot, so maybe shorts. Oh wait, we can't wear shorts right now. A dress. No. I don't like dresses. They can see too much. I want to wear jeans. But what top? I don't like any of our tops. They are so boring. I should just pick a color and go with that. Black. I like black tops the best. A t-shirt. The one that hides my hips. Ugh, my hips. Why didn't I exercise?

I just think we need to lose five pounds. Only in spots. Our thighs. They aren't perfectly straight along our body. They should be. I need to make sure I exercise tomorrow. If I could just figure out which one can do all this stuff I want to do, maybe I wouldn't be such a failure.

Why won't they talk to me? I never seem to know what's going on. I just feel horrible all the time. Like if I could figure out how all this works, then we can fix it. Tell me! Someone tell me!

I know she hears them sometimes. Why can't I? Maybe they don't even like me.

IT'S no wonder I hate myself. Even the other ones won't talk to me, and they are *all* me, well *her*. Me. I'm in better shape than she is, right?

She can't even sleep without me. So I must be doing something she needs. What though? Oh no, she's uncomfortable. Why? Is something wrong? Why is she moving so much? Did I miss something? Was she moving the whole time I was trying to figure out what to wear? Something must be wrong!

―――

ALISA 4:53 am

"Hush little baby don't you cry. You know what's going to happen when you close your eyes."

Please someone help me. Please. I'm so cold. I can't see anything. Is he coming?

―――

JESSIE 4:56 am

Amazing grace, how sweet the sound, that saved a wretch like me. I once was lost, but now I'm found.

…Was blind, but now I *see*.
Just keep singing. It'll all be okay. Just keep singing.

―――

HER *5:14 am*

LETZIE 8:05 am

I hate alarm clocks. I should change that sound to something else. Maybe I'll want to get up then. Get up. Get up. Come on. Get up.

Okay, I'm up. Need coffee. I can probably sit for a minute and play my game. I don't need an hour to get ready. I can make it. I just need a minute to relax. Coffee. I need coffee. Normal people drink coffee in the morning.

I shouldn't be playing this game. I need to get ready. Ugh, why didn't I figure out what to wear today? What is the weather going to be like? Seriously, hot! I guess I could wear shorts. No, can't. Dress code at work. It's too hot for jeans. I hate dresses. I just want jeans. I can make those work.

Get up. Go pick out some jeans.

Which jeans? Why are there so many choices? I don't like any of these. Why aren't any of my clothes cute? This is stupid. If I could just stay home, I would probably be happier. I wouldn't have to figure out what to wear everyday. I wouldn't always have to rush. I could just relax. Stay away from people.

I hate people. Why don't I have a job where there aren't any people? Someone is probably going to irritate me today. I'll probably get yelled at for something stupid. People are stupid.

What! I only have ten minutes? How did that happen? Ugh, why was I wasting my time playing that game? I guess these jeans are fine. Oh my word, oh my word, oh my word, which shirt? Pick a shirt! Just throw one on! I hate this shirt! Why do I even own this shirt?

I hate this shirt too!

No.
No.
No.

Three minutes! Oh my word, I have to be ready *now*. I haven't even done my makeup or my hair! I still have to put milk in my coffee. I hate myself. I hate my life. I'm so stupid.

―――

GEE 8:58 am

Late for work again. What the heck? Good thing I drive fast!

I need some driving music. Something fast with a good beat. Yes. This song rocks. Turning it up loud. Crack the windows. Sun is out. I'm feeling good.

Two minutes late, all is good. No one will notice. Just pretend you aren't late, and don't point it out. Be all cheery. I got this.

―――

SAVANNAH 9:03 am

My to-do list is crazy. How am I going to finish this? Why doesn't anyone else that works here see all this stuff that needs to get done? I'm so irritated. There is no way I'll be able to get all this done today.

Let me see what I can delegate. Making a list. Okay, I'll feel better when a few of these get crossed off. I'm awesome at my job.

I can do this.

Who Am I?

THE NEVER-ENDING QUESTION OF "WHO AM I?"

There are four-hundred and thirty-six of me. Maybe only one hundred. Or thirty. Or several thousand.

I am programmed.

I am completely normal.

I am always confused.

I am invincible.

Asking myself who I am does not reap a reward for me. I get so many answers. I feel differently. Sometimes every other minute, sometimes I can feel like I am the same for days. Other times I live happily for months before I realize anything has changed.

The answer to "Who am I?" is: "I do not know."

I Am The One
JUNE 23RD, 2013

I am the one who belongs.

I can control who is out and I can send them back.

That is what you all need to learn... to be in control of who is out.

The crazy woman's warning (*in church*): *She* is the kind that is dangerous. *She* is a reminder of why we must be careful who we say what to. People like *her*.

My sense is that she is a demon in disguise placed in church to wreak havoc. Or maybe it is simply fear leading my thoughts astray.

God sees our hearts, not our mistakes.

People.

I have long believed God is all I need and I have walked in that belief. My belief that *He* is my saving grace has both saved me and brought unhealthy habits with it.

If you believe you need no one but God, then the relationships you choose to have suffer the consequences. There is no investment. You use people until your need changes and then you move on.

But God is about relationships.

God is about love.

Believing God is all you need *is* the truth. He puts people in your life who need you, that you need, who teach you, and that grow you.

Living superficially means you never grasp the true meaning of love, or the lesson, the deep healing, the peace, or the joy that comes from enmeshing yourself in a gift God has given you... love.

some of US

YOU SPEND HOURS ATTEMPTING TO CREATE AN EXPLANATION that makes sense. One that is *explainable*. You crave answers. *Truth*. Anything to calm the chaos of insanity living this life makes you feel.

You categorize and have no idea if you are right.

Who is the Main? The Host?

Is the name chosen for these books real? Is there an Avah?

There are Protectors: They eliminate threat and take the pain. I know *this* is true.

There are rational ones but they don't seem to have a good grasp on life.

The Self-Destroyer is real. I constantly fight thoughts of self-harm, either upon myself, or happening to women I do not really see or know.

There are sexual alters. So many of them. To face an act I struggle with more than any other. For obvious reasons. Being married makes this a battle. Not only for myself, but out of love for my husband. It is a tragic end to sexual trauma, constantly fighting what should not be something you fear.

There are children. I have *so* many young ones. They were created in droves, it seems. Lots of them never aged. They are stuck at the age I created them, never allowed enough life to grow.

I have Emotions. Literally. Alters created to *be* emotions. Fear. Anger. Rage. Hatred. Sorrow. Pain.

There is a Robot. We think her name is Galaxy now. She took the abuse. It's easier to convince your mind you did the things that happened to you because you were nothing more than a robot and were programmed to.

Penelope has introduced herself once. She is twelve years old. I do not know her purpose.

Annabelle lives in darkness, between worlds. She is numb and not fully a person in any world.

An is a peacemaker and a protector.

Genevieve is chaotic and she cuts people off. Thankfully, she has eliminated many unhealthy people from my life.

Rebekah is a broken, suicidal child. She terrifies me when she is out, because she is strong. She wants nothing more than for her pain to end. She is convinced death will take away her pain. She is no longer allowed out.

Kelly is a protector and very defensive.

They all whisper of their existence and give me little or nothing of who they are.

Shelby is a homeless girl, and a yeller.

One has allergies and another heart issues.

I am convinced a whole lot of them have British accents. When I talk to myself when I am alone, it is almost always in an accent.

SHELBY:

She handles details. I asked her to tell me some of

them… she told me the reason I sometimes hear nothing when I ask is because I have Scramblers.

(*I do not know if this is the same Shelby mentioned above*).

―――――

FAITH:

Dec 2012

My name is Faith. I've only just received a name. I've been living as one of the main hosts for a long time. Jesus gave me my name. He said 'Faith creates butterflies.'

They are beautiful: pastel ones. Alters that will learn to fly to freedom, set free from pain and darkness.

I have love, and faith. Faith that things will become better, whole.

It is this lesson I must teach the others… teach the main, so she may begin to live.

So we can all be whole.

―――――

ANGELICA

Her name is Angelica and she is fierce.

There is attitude in her eyes. She is pretty. Sassy. She'll take nothing from anyone and smirk at anyone who doesn't meet her approval.

She tends to like shock value and will answer just to see what response she will get, even if she knows it really isn't appropriate.

She is fun to be around. She likes rap with catchy beats. Club music played loudly. Don't bother with the music that puts you to sleep.

Ask her to go and do something and you will get a yes, because she likes to be social and enjoys a crowd.

ANNABELLE
April 2nd, 2013
She is twelve years old.
She is childish and thinks lots of things are funny. She giggles a lot, like she knows things others do not.

REBEKAH
May 23rd, 2012
This entry was written by Rebecca and another alter (handwriting changed) explaining for her, to me, why she was out.
I was raped. By ——————-.
She is hurt, afraid, suicidal, lost, alone.
(She cries, and cries, and cries).
She is desperate for a way to make herself feel better. Pills, cutting, death.
The trigger for this tidbit of information: The hubby adjusted the covers on both of us and then got back into bed.

A journal scribble
JAN 18TH, 2014

DURING PRAYER/WORSHIP

I saw myself put my head down and start screaming.

I stepped outside of myself,

inside of myself to comfort an alter.

Definitive shift.

It felt like I was literally splitting.

Such an uncomfortable feeling.

I was aware that a lot of alters were up front listening and watching, and trying to understand.

Kindness
DEC 2012

Sometimes kindness can be too much.

The knowledge that someone knows me enough to understand, to see who I am.

That they might know me.

It hurts.

I struggle with it.

It's a different kind of pain. It changes things in my head.

It makes it harder to stay.

The Parts

I AM SEPARATE. SPLIT IN HALF.

One half of me tries to live. The other is dead.

There is nothing.

They look out from blank eyes that feel the deadness that clings to us like snow that never stops falling.

We are numb.

The half that knows this is not life cannot break through. We see the others looking back, feel them holding too tight, and hear them protest that every thought is unbearable.

End it, they whisper. *Make it stop*.

We do not know how.

Thin
JUNE 23RD, 2013

THIN IS IMPORTANT.

I crave it.

Perfection is a goal, and unhealthy or not, I crave it. But it sits in my mind... a thought only some of us act on because others know it will destroy us if it becomes a goal for all of us.

Sliver of the Droplet

The blood that falls and drips like rain.
I see the truth before it disappears again.
It whispers taunts
like an evil spore.
It digs out fear and molds it into more.

Nightmares
JAN 30, 2013

I HAD A NIGHTMARE (MEMORIES?) LAST NIGHT.

In the dream, I was moving into a new house and found a second kitchen that was closed off from the rest of the house, but as I was exploring it I realized there was food in the cupboards and the fridge; fresh (like milk).

There was a woman there and I thought it was me (I don't remember why) but then I realized she wasn't me and I looked in the mirror and saw that we were two different people (I think she was an alter).

Once I realized she was not me, she warned me, strongly, to leave.

Then I was lying on my back on the floor and I felt fear and a force came in. Not a person, but an evil presence.

It raped me. I was screaming, but no sound was coming out (because my voice was stolen). I turned my head and there was a child lying on the floor next to me. I was horrified to see that it was my sister.

The dream shifted and I was trying to get out of a different house. I jumped through a glass window into water.

A man saw me jump.

I was looking for a place to hide.

I entered a building and asked for clothes... then fuzziness. When I was screaming in the dream, I had the impression I was clawing at the sheets and really screaming... except just like in the dream, no sound was coming from my mouth.

My hubby said he did not hear me through all of this. I know I was awake. His hand was right there next to me, but I could not reach it to wake him. I could not move at all. I was lost in the nightmare.

My daughter had a nightmare the same night. She woke me up and snuggled with me for a bit.

I am horrified this morning about the dream. I believe I was raped by a demon in my past, or that the demon was possibly a possessed person. It is possible my mind simply made the face into something else to protect myself.

I am also afraid my sister suffered through more than she or I remember. Perhaps that is a blessing for both of us.

A Poem

Found in my writings from middle school

An unforgiving emotion
    tears at my heart.
    Claws at my body,
    rips me apart.
    It tears at my skin,
    sucking out my blood
    and it sinks into a pool as deep as a flood.

My hands cup my wounds as tears slip down my face,
    and suddenly, the creatures vanish…
    are gone without a trace.

My screams break the silence,
    startle me awake.
    I stare into the Darkness
    and dwell on the nightmares my mind creates.

Bad Dreams

ONE:

The daughter was taken.

I searched and searched. I did not give up.

It took a month to find her.

She had been severely abused and broken and disease-ridden. AIDS.

The two men that had her also had the disease. Horrible.

―――

TWO:

Tornado.

Came for all of us.

I saw bridges falling and we jumped into the water to try and save ourselves.

Things fell in the water and pushed us under.

The daughter was under for awhile and when we brought her up she had a nail in her head.

We pulled it out (it was shallow) and there was blood, but we were all alive.

I don't remember if there was an end.
FEAR

MORE DREAMS

July 4th, 2013 week
Vacation in cabin up north

I'm tired of bad dreams.
NIGHT ONE: DREAM ONE:

I was running from someone. I was trying to hide but everywhere I hid, people could see me. It seemed like a long dream and I tried to hide in a lot of different places.

The building I was in was large and I remember a lot of black walls.

The last place I tried to hide was outside, on some metal thing out in the open.

The theme of the dream was that it didn't matter where I tried to hide, it was impossible; someone could always see me.

NIGHT ONE: DREAM TWO:

I only remember there was a rape and I felt the physical pain of it.

NIGHT TWO: DREAM ONE:

I was looking for a shower in this huge house. A rich guy and his son lived there and I think I was on vacation.

There was a huge room of showers and the father and the son were each in a spacious one and all that was left were tiny box showers. All of them had sort of see-through doors so I found one away from the front in a corner that was in a branch-off of the room I think (like a gym).

I was in the shower and the water suddenly started to drown me. It was in my face and any way I turned to try and get away, it was choking me and pounding onto me so I could not breathe. I couldn't get out and had to fight. When I finally broke free I was bleeding, bruised and exhausted.

I was dragging myself along the ground, saying "help" but I could barely hear myself.

NIGHT TWO: DREAM TWO:

I was in a store and S——- comes up to me with birthday presents.

There were other people but I don't know who they were.

She made me open the presents in the store.

The first one was a jewelry box with two layers and lots of little squares with different pieces of jewelry in each one that she had personally picked out.

When I tried to close the box to open the next gift it wouldn't close and all of the jewelry was getting jumbled and falling out.

I remember picking up a lot of single jewelry pieces and I don't remember if I ever opened the other gifts.

LAST NIGHT OF VACATION:

Was fine until we were in the cabin and going to bed.

I was settled when suddenly there was COMPLETE CHAOS in my head.

I was freaking out!

I tried desperately to calm myself down, begging an alter to come out and sleep so I could stop it.

At one point I was demanding that a sleeper come out and then I heard *'we're in the woods, don't you know what happens in the woods?'*

Panic.

I asked *'what?'* and told them to tell me.

Then there was an obvious physical and mental switch. An came out.

All was peaceful and calm.

She took us to sleep and she is gone this morning.

I feel yucky.

BREATHE

Fear of darkness pervades,
    striking me at odd moments.
    I feel like crying,
    but if I do, I am afraid my tears will never stop.
    I catch my breath.
    I am terrified if I let it out,
    all of it will come out,
    released on an exhale to fill the air around me.
    Until there is nothing left to breathe.
    Nothing left but suffocation.
    Of the truth.

Offering

I turn my eyes away.

I turn my eyes away from the truth that demands to be seen.

To be seen is to acknowledge denial no longer exists.

Denial no longer exists as memories flood forward from behind locked doors.

Locked doors that hold tight secrets of a past I forgot.

I forgot that the face, *your face*, has destroyed my denial, and brings only pain.

Pain I burrowed deep beneath my skin so I could survive.

I could survive if I did not remember the havoc that was wrought.

Wrought like the veins throughout my body, parallel veins of pain.

Pain sparking like fire now and catching hold to burn.

Burning away the satisfying quench of ignorance you have stolen.

You have stolen my denial as easily as you destroyed my soul.

My soul that I had to encircle with others to be alive.

To be alive was a notch in denial's belt, a facade I believed.

I believed I was existing in my life, that I lived with a modicum of contentment.

A modicum of contentment was preferable.

Preferable to knowing.

Knowing entwines me to you, grasps us together as though your hand holds mine.

Your hand holds mine in the memories, a soft smile upon your lips.

Upon your lips you paint words that suffocate my ears.

My ears hear a lie that has so oft stolen young souls.

Young souls whose innocence is tangible and awakes cravings in those like you.

Those like you who devour innocence like an offering of decadence .

An offering of decadence that was never given.

An offering of decadence that once had so much to offer.

Memories
JAN 31ST, 2013

I remembered in the early morning hours that I wanted to run away when I was very young. Younger than seven, because we first moved when I was that age.

I remember looking at the woods beyond the field and thinking no one would find me there.

Seven-year-olds do not typically want to run away. Significant... obviously, something was wrong.

I also used to eat out of the dog/cat food bowl. Did my parents feed me?

More questions:

There is something about the cellar. Or the basement. I don't even know if there was one.

Piano... was there a hole behind it with caves? What a crazy thought.

Did I really try to cut off my brothers finger?

I wet the bed for a long time... a signal of abuse.

My mother ran over my cat. I always believed it was on purpose.

IT IS SO frustrating to have so many little fragments and have no one to ask about them. I have cut myself off from the majority of my family to protect myself.

I do not know who my abusers are. I have suspicions, and some concrete proof of things, but for the most part, the secret of *who* is hidden from me. I may never remember. I have tried to, thinking it would be easier.

I'm no longer sure I agree. If my mind hides truths, I have come to accept it is because I would not be able to handle what is there and survive.

My brain has invested an incredible amount of time and energy into survival. I live my entire life out of the strategy it used to do so.

So I will not think about the basements. Or the missing rooms. Or the faceless people and their shadows and the fear that fighting to see their faces causes.

Where I am right now will have to be enough.

Until I am stronger and can take another step forward toward healing.

Toward being whole.

Self-reflection
MAY 20TH, 2008

What I have learned from this life:

———

One of me was bipolar.

    I never felt loved.

    I have a support system if I choose to trust people around me.

    Trust is difficult because I expect people to let me down.

    God is powerful.

    I used to be reactive and not proactive. I am still reactive a lot.

    I can not sustain without relaxation. This is highly important for my well-being.

    I learned I have never loved myself.

    I learned the hubby loves me enough to stand by me under horrible circumstances.

    Sleep is vital to my health, and lots of it.

    I have sensory issues. SO many!

    My mind is truly scary.

———

2020

    Life is not all bad.

    There are good people left in this world.

    Happiness and joy are actually real.

    I am strong. Not fearless, but I have a surprising amount of resilience.

Belief is an action.

Acceptance when you live as a DID survivor is constant and necessary, and hardly ever is full acceptance. You just get comfortable bouncing from one 'okay whatever' to the next. It also, in my experience, gets easier.

I doubt it's a good skill to learn; sometimes shrugging and setting things into a box in my mind is probably not acceptance, but avoidance.

Acceptance and avoidance are very similar.

I'm mostly happy. The 'blips' as I call them now, are still frequent and annoying, but they no longer take over my life.

Journal Entry
MAY 1ST, 2008

I WOKE UP CRAZY TODAY.

So much energy it made me feel euphoric.

I did laundry and then got ready for exercise class and I needed ankle socks. I was throwing clothes everywhere; grabbing what I wanted and making a mess.

I jumped on the hubby to wake him up. Smiled. He said *'you're happy today.'*

I ran around the house looking for ankle socks, went to the store and bought some and sang a song while I was walking down the aisles. People were looking at me like I was nuts.

I was calm for my massage, manic for my therapy session, and calm again when I stood in line for three-and-a-half hours at a store, then left without buying anything because I didn't want to miss my other exercise class.

This class calmed me down. I noticed a big difference. I went out. My favorite DJ was there but that feeling of euphoria I'd had during the morning was gone.

IT'S GONE. Now, I'm just here.

I liked it even though it made me FEEL crazy.

I miss it already.

It's better than the other, where I just keep wondering when I'm going to die.

Being Alone
JAN 31ST, 2014

Survival is not living.

There's a comfort that comes from being alone. Knowing no one will walk in, no one will disturb the silence that allows complete freedom to be exactly what each moment is.

A song might break out. Words that make no sense. Sudden dances or giggles.

No one will question anything I do if they can't see me. Freedom.

Mostly, the soothing magnitude of being alone becomes apparent when darkness has fallen. It is, after all, the biggest trigger of all. When there are others, it is missed. A lost shift amongst stimuli.

Coca-Cola

IN A MEETING:

Feeling very agitated. Too much stimulus.

It is taking too long.

I need to get out, but I won't.

I don't know if it is me or her that wants to leave?

Finally, we broke for lunch.

I saw a Coca-Cola.

I all but flipped out (we were not drinking it at this time).

I had to have one, but I was very upset it was there. And then I knew.

They gave it to me as a baby.

I began to cry.

S———— was there. I turned around and told her I had to leave *right* now.

I went outside. She came with me and talked until my host came back.

*I think they drugged the Coca-Cola.

COFFEE

WHAT THE H——- IS WRONG WITH COFFEE?

No one is taking away my coffee. It may not be okay for you, but it's a necessary thing for me. who cares why. I need it. You want to survive? drink the coffee.

not hot chocolate. Not tea. COFFEE COFFEE COFFEE I will not explain it to you. not your business. make the d——- coffee

drink it

as much as you want

HOME

I am most comfortable inside of these walls, enshrouding me with shades drawn… no eyes can see in and steal my safety, a well constructed haven that holds me in and keeps me whole.

Darkness falls, a peaceful comfort to lend aid— soft blankets and wool socks and fluffy pillows, all not allowed outside these brick and mortar walls.

Daylight spills, light shines in and I panic, pulling forgotten drapes and coverings to ensure that only artificial light will lend its life upon the familiarity of my furnishings…

the wooden gleam of my table, the soft cushion and blanket on my favorite space to unwind.

Swirls of color on the rug, easy flow of rustic along the walls. They are mine, set there to remind me that I chose this place.

I prefer to be locked inside of these doors, each room a beacon of self that keeps everything outside my own world, pieces of my soul that even in need of improvement is still who I am and uses no words or emotion to scar me further.

Outside these walls the chaos I feel when I am not home erupts with unkempt, uneven, in-need-of-care places I avoid.

Weeds and jagged lines that offer no smoothness, no respite, rocks tumbled carelessly along the path that leads me away from safety, away from comfort, into the world that lends credence to my yearning to seek my spaces that are me, that I know, and that are familiar.

Eyes that are windows see too much, are too close, drive by to mock me, no tall statues with strong branches to shield me, noise bleeding in to push my mind, desperate for peace, into folds of smooth warm comfort and plush curves.

Chosen eyes and noise on screen that block out the invading world, brought in when I give it power, seeking distraction, muddling me back into the haven of security that I call home, cocooned inside of my favorite blanket, hugged by my favorite chair, surrounded by all that is me.

The Screaming of the Others
2018

I OFTEN DREAM OF SILENCE.

The simplicity of being alone is a privilege that eludes me. Others share my space, and offer up snippets of conversation that leak into my consciousness, a constant chatter behind the scenes that rings in my ears, and echoes in my head.

It isn't a delusion, or a mental illness. My stability is a partial question based on functionality, and as a high- functioning individual, logic places me firmly on the scale of normal.

It's intriguing when they (the others) answer a question that I've already answered, but *their* response is different. A pause in my core, a slight tilt of my head while I listen, asking the redundant question "*Was that real?*"

It always is. I've learned the cycle of denial is a lifelong battle, that I must always remember past events that re-light the truth, a brightly colored red tack on the "*we've been here*" map.

Now, I most often choose to chuckle at the contradictions, while before I would have been cast into a depressive haze of confusion. My answer, as the host personality, rules. I am the one in control and they are the orphans I hold under my wing.

I am what you call DID. An individual with Dissociative Identity Disorder, more commonly known as Multiple Personality Disorder.

It's not the scary depiction Hollywood so enjoys portraying.

It's a simple, impossibly complex defense mechanism employed to survive from consistent trauma. Sometimes it's easier for me to call it PTSD, or a story I created that became real, or even nothing more than a dream.

Some days are harder than others. A self dialogue about existence and truth and lies. Easier days, the past fades deep into the background and allows me to live, with minimal feedback from the others.

I've come forth from a place of dark self-hatred, a war against myself as I broke through thick concrete walls erected by the others to protect me from the truth, but that became the opposite of what they intended.

Protecting me stole my sanity. A mind fractured into pieces that do not fit together cannot be explained. The pieces need to be re-shaped, re-painted, re-pictured, until they become pieces of the same puzzle.

We first had to begin to work together, allowing our stories to be shared, accepted, and felt. Pain without explanation causes more pain. It is not until you understand the cause of the pain that true healing can begin.

That is how they speak now. *To* me. Not *at* me. Where before they screamed to be heard, now they *are* heard. I hear them. I listen. *I* choose what to do with what they say. *I* choose how to answer.

They have always been versions of me. Created for a purpose, locked away until I could begin to understand. The goal is to become *one* me, but until then, I have mostly accepted their presence.

Sometimes their words and their knowledge hurt. Those days can become a series of days where the one speaking rises to the surface enough that we share the space and both (or several) of us struggle to go through the motions of life.

My functionality decreases greatly during those times. My voice fades into silence, my emotions alternate between extreme or lacking. A sheer curtain falls, hazing my view of life and stealing my peace. The chatter becomes deafening, a cacophony of static that I cannot differentiate into anything that makes sense.

Years ago, these battles were fought with prescription pills, cutting, and dark depression that often lasted months while I fought the constant urge to end my life.

I have become adept at shutting down for only days now, at recognizing that someone has come forward to speak, then listening. Giving them a voice, acknowledging what they endured so we could live, feeling the pain, and then rising above it.

I embrace them as best I can, and sometimes they choose to dissolve into me, to allow me to take over the part of me they were created to be.

I cannot resent them. I created them. I gave them a voice. A purpose. I must let them speak now, or I take away the core of who we all are. One. One puzzle made up of many, many pieces.

About the Author

Avah Rivers is quite happy living her life now. There's still more than one sharing the space in her head, but she is happy to report she hardly ever loses time to them anymore.

Occasionally, one will say something startling, or get triggered to the surface, but the disruption this used to cause has been almost reduced to zero. Her husband and the child still living at home might argue differently, but according to Avah, all is well.

A praise report, to be sure. Avah has high hopes her progress toward healing will continue without the dark suffering she remembers. Feeding the others Cheetohs, hamburgers and french fries seems to help.

Acknowledgments

To every person who learned the truth and nodded their heads and verbally stated the annoying phrase: "so much makes sense now."

Thanks for deciding to still love me anyway.

Also by Avah Rivers

The Octobers

The Shadows That Hide Me

Printed in Great Britain
by Amazon